GUIDE TO SUCCESS

CRESTLINE BOOKS

This book is dedicated to my friends, family and all those hustling to make money online daily.

Contents

CHAPTER ONE

Self-Discipline as a Sure Way to Success

Here are some tips to help you stay on course and develop more self-discipline in all aspects of your life.

- Understand that the choices you make in life are yours and yours alone, you can't blame others for your failure if you lack self-discipline
- If you make mistakes in life, learn by them, pick yourself up and practice being more self-disciplined with yourself in the future
- Set yourself realistically achievable goals, once you have written out your goals make sure that you do everything in your power to stick to them and achieve them. Goals go a long way to encouraging you to discipline yourself.
- Always finish any task you set about doing before moving on to start another
- Avoid temptation from others around you to deviate from what it is you want to achieve, they may lack self-discipline but don't be swayed to following their ways
- Taking up a new sport, particularly one that requires a lot of self-discipline to excel at is an excellent way of improving yourself
- Notice the benefits you have gained from practicing self-discipline, keeping a journal is an excellent way of achieving this
- Imagine the consequences that being un-disciplined brings
- Your willpower is at its lowest when you feel stressed so take it easy, learn how to relax
- Take notice of when and why you start to go off track and deviate, again a journal can help you to keep track of these times

- Use affirmations to help you in times when you are frustrated or doubt yourself

CHAPTER TWO

How to be successful in life

We all want to be successful in life but what can we do to assure that success, succeeding in life isn't as hard as you might think, there isn't any secret to it but rather just common sense, positive thinking and attitude, and initiative. Along with this knowledge and understanding here are some tips to guide you down the path of success.

- Persevere – perseverance and determination are what is needed for success, if you don't give up on something you attempt then you can't fail, it's as simple as that. If something doesn't work out as planned the first time then try and try again using different methods to achieve the result that you are looking for.
- Change – if you are not happy with what you have now, or who you are in life then the only one that can make a difference to your situation or life is you. A change could mean changing your outlook on life, your outlook on yourself, your priorities, or your activities, you have no one else to blame but yourself and only you have the power to change.
- What goes around comes around – you only get back in life what you are willing to put into it, if you are helpful, honest, truthful, and positive then you will get the same back in return which can help you on your path to success, particularly in the workplace.
- You cannot succeed alone – all successful people rely in part on others for their success, every person has different skills, talents, and abilities which when combined leads to an individual's success.
- Center yourself – we all need to take time out during the day to center ourselves, by re-focusing ourselves and what we wish to achieve we can accomplish more and be more effective in our tasks.

- Set yourself targets or goals – setting out targets or goals for yourself can help you to succeed in anything you choose, these can be daily, short-term or long-term targets with the short term being a month or so and the long term no longer than 6 months. Always set realistic targets and give yourself a date by which to reach your target, review your targets regularly to make sure they are always attainable.
- Don't strive for perfection – never try to be perfect, no one is perfect, set a standard and goal and do the task or job to the very best of your ability and be happy with that, as long as you gave it your best shot that's all you or anyone else can ask for.
- Believe in yourself – develop strategies that make you more aware of yourself and what you are capable of achieving, if you believe in yourself and what you are capable of achieving then you are more likely to be successful in whatever you do.
- Focus on what you won't – focus on the positive and what it is you want to achieve instead of the negative or what it is that you don't want to achieve, always look ahead instead of back and focus only on the desired result.

CHAPTER THREE

Top 10 Time Management Skills

Tips for managing your time more efficiently

- Break down large tasks into smaller ones and tackling each part one at a time can ease the stress considerably than facing one larger task
- Get rid of routine tasks, if a task is done just out of routine instead of necessity then eliminate it if possible.
- Look at your habits to see if they could be changed, maybe you could do certain things in different ways and save yourself some time in the process.
- Evaluate yourself to determine if you are a morning person or night person and organize tasks to use whatever time suits you best.
- Learn to say the word "no" when asked to do something for someone, don't be continually put upon by others who know you cannot refuse them, it's ok doing favors but it can take considerable time from your day.

Top 10 Time Management Skills

The secret to managing time successfully is being able to manage yourself, although we often think we don't waste a minute of our time, in reality, this is far from true and there are many ways which we can manage ourselves more efficiently which ultimately leads to more successful time management. To successfully manage time there are strategies that you can use to stay more in control and relieve stress which plays a big factor in successful time management.

1. Attempting to do too much – in today's busy world many people want things done yesterday and this only leads to rushing around and not doing a task properly, it also leads to mistakes and half-finished work with no real feeling of having accomplished anything with your time.
2. A lack of priorities – this is the single biggest cause of time-wasting, to successfully manage the time we have to know exactly what our priorities are for the day, by not prioritizing we spend too much time on the minor things and not enough time on the important ones.
3. Interruptions – we all get interruptions in our day, this could be someone dropping in and asking if you have a minute to spare, which usually turns into a half-hour or more. Knowing how to successfully deal with interruptions in your daily life is essential to time management.
4. Procrastination – thinking about what you have to do instead of getting on and doing it is one of the biggest time wasters in your day, reduce the amount of time that you spend thinking and this leaves you more time for doing.
5. Learn to say "no" - many of us just cannot say the words "no" when asked if we mind doing something, this is usually out of fear of upsetting the other person, but if you are taking on the responsibilities of others then you are taking time away from your workload or tasks and essentially robbing yourself of that precious time which leads to stressing you out.
6. Clutter – look around your desk or workspace, do you know where everything is? If you are asked for a file can you lay your hands on it or do you have to go rummaging to find it? a cluttered desk or workspace is a time-waster.
7. Set deadlines for yourself – work out a reasonable deadline for a particular project and make sure that you stick with the deadline.
8. Manage your e-mails and phone calls - where possible manage when you read your e-mails and take phone calls better, this was you are not continually breaking off to answer a call or reply to an e-mail. Set aside certain times when you check your e-mail and reply to them, the same applies to phone calls, it is surprising how much time can be wasted throughout a day by stopping and starting a project or task.
9. Use an activity planner – setting your day out in a planner can help you save time, a planner will allow you to allocate tasks to time slots, and this

way you can plan your day out and maximize your time more efficiently.

10. Avoid multi-tasking – starting many different projects at the same time is not a very efficient way of managing time, try to complete one project before starting on another, this gives you the satisfaction of seeing the project complete and knowing you have accomplished something with your time.

CHAPTER FOUR

Improving Your Listening Skills

To be able to communicate successfully with others we have to develop our listening skills, truly listening to what someone is saying and understanding them is the key to effective communication. While the majority of us think we listen to what others are saying, in fact very few of us do listen intently and this is where misunderstandings can arise, which leads to difficulties and sometimes arguments.

Most of us have, over the years developed poor listening habits and have continued through life with these habits, some of the most common habits that people have developed which lead to poor listening skills include.

- Listening without really hearing what the other is saying, often leaves us missing the point
- We allow other influences around us to distract us and drift away from the conversation
- We pretend we are listening when in fact we are thinking of something else and only hear snatches of what is being said
- Very often start out listening then if we think we know what is being said, interrupt the person before they have finished talking
- A person can often hear what they want to hear, or what they think they should be haring which is often very different from what is being said
- We often assume we know why something is being said and jump on the defensive side
- We can't wait for an opportunity to butt into the conversation with our point of view

These are the most common mistakes that many of us make when it comes to listening, or rather, not listening. However by realizing your mistakes and attempting to change them, you are more likely to be aware of your mistakes, and this makes changing bad habits easier. To develop positive and effective listening habits you should follow the following tips.

- Even if what the talker is saying is boring, you have to force yourself to listen intently to what they are saying and not be tempted to drift away into your world. As well as focusing on what they are saying, watch their body languages such as eye contact, hand movements, and head nods.
- Listen to everything they are saying even if this means acknowledging the unpleasant or what you don't particularly want to hear.
- Try not to draw any conclusion before you have heard everything the person is saying to you, don't butt into the conversation before they have finished by guessing what they are going to say.
- Question the speaker in a non-judgmental way, by asking questions in this manner you will very often find that what the speaker has in mind and what you assumed are two different things.
- When unsure ask them directly if what you think is actually what they meant, this can very often alleviate or stop any misunderstandings from occurring.

The more you practice improving your listening skills the easier it becomes until you develop these new habits as second nature. You will then find that you get along with people easier and are less likely to get into conflicts through misunderstandings.

CHAPTER FIVE

Exercises and Success

Individuals of all ages must get the right amount of exercise daily. However, it's particularly crucial that senior men and women also engage in regular exercise to maintain suitable health and fitness.

As we age, the body starts to decelerate a little bit, affecting assorted aspects of our health. Particularly, our muscle strength, endurance, and flexibility start to suffer. When you pass the age of twenty-five, your total body strength diminishes by 4% each decade. This may make it more and more difficult to take part in daily activities, like household cleaning, meal prep, and social events. Regular exercise may help to combat the loss of this muscle strength and return much-needed flexibility and endurance.

A lot of seniors decide against regular exercise as they're afraid that it might be dangerous for them. While senior citizens might not wish to get involved in activities like rock climbing or endurance contests, it's perfectly safe for the majority of seniors to take part in moderate physical activities. To be on the safe side, though, make certain to check with your doctor before you start any sort of exercise routine. However, most doctors recommend that senior citizens try to get the least half-hour of exercise daily, even if they're suffering from particular age-related health disorders.

Senior citizens must pursue a combination of separate physical activities to get the level best health benefits possible. When you decide to start an exercise routine, there are a few things that you ought to keep in mind.

Most importantly, it's crucial to assess your level of conditioning. If you haven't been exercising regularly, you must start slowly. Kickoff with only 5 or 10 minutes of exercise at a time, and take regular breaks. You may slowly build your exercise routine as your body gets accustomed to the exercise.

Likewise, make certain to pick an activity or exercise that's correct for you. Pick activities that are fun to do and that will keep you interested. And never perform an exercise that causes you painfulness. Low-intensity, easy activities are always best.

www.ingramcontent.com/pod-product-compliance
Ingram Content Group UK Ltd.
Pitfield, Milton Keynes, MK11 3LW, UK
UKHW021926190726
13853UKWH00002B/874